TABLE CONTENT

Introduction:

Russia annexed Crimea from Ukraine in 2014, and a conflict broke out in Eastern Ukraine. The unfolding events shocked the world and prompted numerous inquiries regarding Russia's intentions and actions in the region. While the contention in Ukraine has numerous mind-boggling factors at play, one huge component that can't be disregarded is the KGB association with the occasions.

Before entering politics, Russia's current president, Vladimir Putin, spent 16 years in the KGB, rising through the ranks to become a Lieutenant Colonel. As the leader of Russia, Putin's background as a KGB agent has shaped his worldview, leadership style, and policies. In this book, we will investigate what Putin's KGB foundation and strategies have meant for the addition of Crimea and the contention in Eastern Ukraine.

We'll look at the Maidan Revolution in Ukraine and the subsequent Russian military intervention that led to the annexation of Crimea. We are going to investigate the conflict that broke out in Eastern Ukraine and the various groups that were involved, such as Ukrainian forces, separatists supported by Russia, and foreign fighters. We will also look into the KGB's role in the conflict, including how their strategies have been used to spread division and advance Russia's objectives.

Also, we will investigate the international response to the events in Ukraine, including the United Nations' role, Western sanctions, and responses from neighboring nations. Last but not least, we will take into account the long-term effects of the conflict in Ukraine and how Putin's actions have affected Russia's relationships with other nations, such as NATO and the United States.

The events in Ukraine have had a significant global impact and will continue to have long-lasting effects. This book aims to shed light on the intricate geopolitical dynamics at work by examining the connection between the KGB and the annexation of Crimea and the conflict in Eastern Ukraine.

Chapter One

Putin's' Early Life and KGB Root

One of the most intriguing and controversial figures of our time is Vladimir Putin. Putin was born in Leningrad, which is now St. Petersburg, in 1952. He came from a working-class family and studied law at Leningrad State University. He joined the KGB, the Soviet Union's intelligence agency, after graduating, where he worked in various capacities for 16 years before entering politics in the early 1990s. With a reputation for being tough, ruthless, and strategic, Putin has since progressed to become one of the most powerful leaders in the world.

Vladimir Putin's early life was shaped by his upbringing in a communal apartment in Leningrad, where he shared a single room with his parents and two siblings. Putin's mother worked in a factory, and his father was a factory foreman. The family lived a life of contentment.

After completing high school, Putin signed up for Leningrad State College, where he studied law.

He decided to pursue a career in intelligence during this time and became interested in the KGB. Putin joined the KGB in 1975 and began his training at the agency's school in Moscow.

Putin was posted to Dresden, East Germany, after completing his training, where he spent five years working as a spy. He learned a lot both personally and professionally during his time in Dresden. Later, he said that it was like a "crash course in reality" where he learned how the real world worked and how to deal with difficult situations.

Putin returned to Leningrad after his assignment in Dresden and continued his KGB career there. He served as a liaison to the Committee for State Security (KGB/C) of the KGB, which was in charge of the Soviet Union's internal security. Putin developed a thorough understanding of the Soviet Union's security apparatus and the strategies it employed to maintain control and suppress dissent while in this position.

Putin gained valuable skills in manipulation and deception during his time with the KGB. He learned how to use his ability to read people and situations to achieve his goals. These abilities would be of great significance to him in his later political vocation.

In 1991, the Soviet Association fell and the KGB was disbanded. Putin was offered a position in the new Russian government, and he accepted. He proceeded to work for the mayor of St. Petersburg and afterward joined the administration of Russian President Boris Yeltsin. In 1999, Yeltsin appointed Putin as prime minister, and when Yeltsin resigned later that year, Putin became acting president. In 2000, he was elected president, and ever since then, he has held power.

Both his early life in a communal apartment and his time working for the KGB have shaped Putin's worldview and leadership style. His upbringing and time spent in the KGB both contributed to his tough, uncompromising style as well as his focus on maintaining control and projecting strength.

Putin gained a thorough understanding of the inner workings of the Russian security apparatus and the significance of maintaining control over key institutions from his time working for the KGB. His approach to governance and foreign policy has been significantly influenced by this knowledge.

Putin's handling of the Ukrainian conflict is one illustration of this. Putin's extension of Crimea and backing for separatists in eastern Ukraine should be visible as a sign of his faith in the significance of keeping up with Russian impact over neighboring countries. This belief stems from his time working for the KGB, where he would have witnessed firsthand the Soviet Union's efforts to keep control over its Eastern European satellite states.

Putin's approach to opposition and dissent is another illustration. Putin has a history of repressing political opponents and limiting press freedom. This should be visible as a continuation of the strategies utilized by the KGB to stifle disagreement and keep up with control during the Soviet period.

Furthermore, Putin's upbringing in the KGB may have played a role in his perception of the West as a threat to Russia. The KGB was tasked with gathering intelligence and countering perceived Western threats during the Cold War. This experience may have influenced Putin's belief that Russia must assert its dominance and respond to what he perceives as Western encroachment.

Exploring Putin's KGB background has provided valuable insights into his leadership style and decision-making processes. It shed light on the elements that have shaped his perspective on the world as well as how he views governance and foreign policy.

CHAPTER 2

The Annexation of Crimea

In this chapter, the annexation of Crimea in 2014 will be discussed. We will investigate the Maidan Revolution in Ukraine, the Crimean referendum, and the subsequent Russian military intervention that led to the annexation.

A significant turning point in the conflict between Russia and Ukraine was the annexation of Crimea. We'll look at the Maidan Revolution in Ukraine, the Crimean referendum, and the Russian military intervention that followed the annexation in this chapter.

Maidan Revolution in Ukraine and the Referendum

Protests and civil unrest in Ukraine occurred in 2013 and 2014 as part of the Maidan Revolution, also known as the Euromaidan Revolution. President Yanukovych's decision to abandon a deal with the European Union in favor of closer ties with Russia sparked the protests. Democratic reforms and closer integration with Europe were among the protesters' demands. The protests eventually turned violent, with confrontations between protesters and law enforcement.

A new government was put in place after Yanukovych was ousted from power in February 2014. Tensions between Russia and Ukraine began to rise as Russia saw the revolution as a threat to its interests in Ukraine. Russia annexed Crimea, a Black Sea peninsula that had been part of Ukraine since 1954, in March 2014. Before the annexation, Crimea held a contentious referendum in which the majority of voters decided to leave Ukraine and join Russia.

Western nations imposed economic sanctions on Russia in response to international condemnation of the annexation of Crimea. Russia, on the other hand, retaliated with its sanctions. In addition, the annexation sparked a conflict in Eastern Ukraine, where separatists supported by Russia took control of several regions.

Within this chapter, we will also examine the role of propaganda and disinformation in the annexation of Crimea. We will analyze the tactics used by Russia and consider their effectiveness in shaping public opinion.

Lastly, we will examine the response of the international community to the annexation of Crimea. We will consider the actions taken by Western countries, including the imposition of economic sanctions, and the response of other countries, including China and Russia's allies. We will also explore the role of international organizations, including the United Nations and NATO, and their response to the crisis in Ukraine.

Role of Propaganda and Disinformation in the Annexation of Crimea.

To gain domestic and international support for the annexation of Crimea and to justify it, the Russian government employed a variety of propaganda strategies. This included making a bogus story of Ukrainian's hostility towards ethnic Russians in Crimea, manipulating social media to create a sense of popular support for the annexation, and spreading false information about the events leading up to the annexation.

Russia's 2014 annexation of Crimea was a significant development in contemporary international relations. It demonstrated the power of propaganda and disinformation to influence public opinion and posed a challenge to the international order that emerged following the Cold War. We will examine the impact of propaganda and disinformation on international relations and the annexation of Crimea further in this chapter.

Governments have long used disinformation and propaganda to sway public opinion and justify their actions. The Russian government used a variety of propaganda strategies to gain domestic and international support for its annexation of Crimea.

The fabrication of a false narrative that Ukraine was attacking ethnic Russians in Crimea was one of Russia's main strategies. The Russian government asserted that the lives and privileges of ethnic Russians in Crimea were in danger from Ukrainian patriots and extremists. This misleading story was utilized to legitimize the Russian military intervention and annexation of Crimea.

One more strategy utilized by Russia was the control of social media to create a sense of popular support for the annexation. Pro-Russian propaganda and false information were disseminated by the Russian government through fake social media accounts. This was done to give the impression that both domestically and internationally, there was widespread support for the annexation.

The Russian government additionally spread false information about the events leading up to the annexation. For instance, it asserted that the protesters in Ukraine were brutal radicals who were undermining the well-being of ethnic Russians in Ukraine. The Russian military intervention and subsequent annexation of Crimea were based on this false information.

The annexation of Crimea's use of propaganda and disinformation had significant effects on international relations. It eroded trust in the mainstream media and created a sense of uncertainty and doubt about the events in Ukraine. This made it hard for Western nations to answer really to the emergency and added to a feeling of division and doubt between Russia and the West.

Moreover, the use of propaganda and misinformation in the annexation of Crimea has wider repercussions for the development of international relations in the years to come. It exemplifies how modern communication technologies can influence public opinion and the course of events. It additionally features the significance of decisive reasoning and media literacy in a time of phony news and disinformation.

All in all, the job of misleading publicity and disinformation in the Annexation of Crimea was significant. The Russian government used a variety of strategies to fabricate a story and gain domestic and international relations. This had significant implications for global relations and highlighted the power of propaganda and disinformation in shaping public opinion. It is important for policymakers, scholars, and the public to be aware of these tactics and to work towards a more informed and critically engaged public discourse.

The tactics used by Russia in the Annexation of Crimea and consider their effectiveness in shaping public opinion.

Russia's 2014 annexation of Crimea was a highly contentious event that challenged the international order established after the Cold War. Russia's use of a variety of strategies to influence public opinion and gain support for its actions was one of the main factors in the annexation's success. We will examine Russia's annexation of Crimea tactics and their effectiveness in influencing public opinion.

The strategies utilized by Russia in the Annexation of Crimea can be extensively separated into two classifications: propaganda and diplomacy, the annexation of Crimea was achieved through diplomacy through the use of military force, and propaganda through the manipulation of information to instill a sense of widespread support for the annexation.

Russia used diplomatic means to accomplish its goals in this circumstance.

The deployment of "little green men," soldiers in unmarked uniforms, to Crimea was one method of diplomacy. This allowed Russia to claim that the soldiers were local self-defense forces and deny that its military was involved in the incident. This strategy was designed to prevent the international community from taking a strong stance against Russia's actions and to buy time for Russia to consolidate its control over Crimea.

Another diplomatic tactic employed by Russia was to hold a referendum in Crimea on joining the Russian Federation. This allowed Russia to present its actions as a response to the will of the people and to legitimize its annexation of the region. However, the legitimacy of this referendum has been widely questioned, and it was not recognized by the international community.

Russia also attempted to shape the narrative of the situation through diplomacy. It claimed that it was defending the rights of ethnic Russians in

Crimea and accused Ukraine of being controlled by "fascists" and "neo-Nazis." Russia sought to gain support from other nations in the region and present itself as a defender of Russian-speaking populations by framing its actions as a response to perceived threats to Russian interests.

Lastly, Russia attempted to avoid or lessen the impact of international sanctions imposed as a result of its actions through diplomacy. It waged a diplomatic campaign to sever ties with China and India, which could potentially provide economic and political support, as well as forge closer ties with the European Union.

Russia's annexation of Crimea relied heavily on diplomacy. It safeguarded Russia's legitimacy in the eyes of the international community while simultaneously reducing the likelihood of direct military conflict. However, it also demonstrated the limitations of diplomacy in the face of a powerful state's aggressive

The response of the international community to the annexation of Crimea.

The annexation of Crimea by Russia in 2014 was met with a strong response from the international community, which saw the activities of Russia as a violation of international law and the territorial integrity of Ukraine. The following are some of the international community's responses to the annexation of Crimea:

Sanctions:

Economic sanctions imposed on Russia were the international community's most significant response to the annexation of Crimea. Both the United States of America and the European Union (EU) imposed sanctions on Russia, focusing on individuals, businesses, and economic sectors. The approvals are expected to seclude Russia monetarily and to come down on the Russian government to pull out from Crimea.

Condemnation: The international community strongly opposed the annexation of Crimea. The Unified Countries General Gathering passed a goal denouncing the extension, with 100 nations casting a ballot in favor, 11 against, and 58 abstentions. Russia's actions were also condemned by the G7, and the EU condemned the annexation and imposed sanctions.

Security measures:

In addition, several nations responded diplomatically to the annexation of Crimea. The US and the EU ousted Russian negotiators and shut down a portion of their departments. Russia's military and practical cooperation with NATO and other nations have both been suspended.

Monetary measures: In response to the annexation of Crimea, some nations also implemented economic measures. Japan suspended some economic cooperation with

Russia, and Canada and Australia both imposed sanctions on Russia.

Military actions:

In response to the annexation of Crimea, some nations increased their military presence in the area. NATO increased its military presence in the Baltic States and Poland, while several European nations and the United States increased their military presence there.

The international community's overall response to the annexation of Crimea was significant and aimed to economically and diplomatically isolate Russia. In addition, the response emphasized the significance of international law and state territorial integrity. However, Russia has maintained its control over Crimea despite the efforts of the international community, and the situation has not been resolved.

Chapter 3

The Conflict in Ukraine

The conflict in Ukraine started at the beginning of 2014, shortly after the Euromaidan revolution toppled Ukraine's pro-Russian President Viktor Yanukovych. Ethnic Russians in eastern Ukraine feared they would be marginalized under the new government, which was pro-Western and anti-Russian. This opposition was met by the new government in Kyiv.

With support from Russia, pro-Russian separatists seized government buildings in Donetsk and Luhansk, proclaimed independence, and established the self-proclaimed Donetsk and Luhansk People's Republics. The Ukrainian military sent off hostile to retake the region, bringing about a fierce clash that has proceeded right up until now.

The people of Ukraine, particularly those living in the eastern regions, have suffered greatly as a result of the conflict. Numerous others have been injured or displaced, and thousands of people have died. The war has destroyed infrastructure and disrupted day-to-day life. Constant shelling and gunfire make it difficult for civilians to obtain food and medical care, two of the most fundamental necessities.

Russia's contribution to the contention has been a subject of extreme worldwide examination. The Russian government has denied direct association, however, proof proposes that Russia has offered military and monetary help to the dissident powers. Russia has also been accused of crossing into Ukraine with troops and weapons.

Russia's relationships with the international community have also been strained as a result of the Ukraine conflict. Energy, finance, and defense are just a few of Russia's key economic sectors that have been hugely affected by economic sanctions the United States and the European Union imposed. NATO has increased its military presence in Eastern Europe by putting troops in Poland and Romania and holding exercises there.

The conflict in Ukraine has not been resolved in spite of international pressure. The fighting has continued despite the failure of the Minsk agreements, which were a ceasefire agreement mediated by France and Germany in 2015. Donetsk and Luhansk are still largely under the control of separatist forces, and there have been occasional acts of violence.

The conflict in Ukraine has wider repercussions for security and international relations. It has prompted a rethink of European security as well as questions about Russia's place in the post-Soviet world. The difficulties of resolving territorial disputes and ethnic tensions in the region have also been brought to light by the conflict.

The world is keeping a close eye out for any indications of a resolution as the conflict in Ukraine continues. The circumstance stays tense, and the fate of the area stays dubious.

The conflict in Ukraine has wider implications for security and international relations. It has prompted a rethink of European security as well as questions about Russia's place in the post-Soviet world. The difficulties of resolving territorial disputes and ethnic tensions in the region have also been brought to light by the conflict.

The issue of Russian aggression in the region has come to the forefront as a result of the conflict in Ukraine. The annexation of Crimea was the first time since The Second Great War that a European nation had annexed another country's territory by force. It has been interpreted as an effort on the part of Russia to expand its sphere of influence in the region and establish its dominance over its neighbors that Russia has been involved in the conflict in Ukraine.

European security has also been reassessed as a result of the conflict. The consensus that Europe had entered a new era of peace and stability following the Cold War has been broken by the annexation of Crimea and the conflict in Ukraine. The contention has prompted a reestablished center around NATO and the requirement for aggregate safeguard against outside dangers.

The difficulties of resolving territorial disputes and ethnic tensions in the region have also been brought to light by the conflict in Ukraine. The east and south of Ukraine have significant Russian-speaking populations, making it a multiethnic nation. Numerous ethnic Russians feel marginalized by the new Kyiv government, which has exacerbated these tensions.

Concerns about how minorities in the region are treated have also been raised by the conflict. Human rights violations, such as torture, extrajudicial killings, and forced disappearances, have been made against both sides. The contention has likewise prompted the removal of millions of individuals, with many escaping to adjoining nations as outcasts.

The international community is having a difficult time finding a solution as the conflict in Ukraine continues. The Minsk agreements, which were supposed to lead to peace and a ceasefire, haven't stopped the fighting. The situation is still tense, and there are concerns that the conflict could get even worse, bringing in additional Countries into the region.

The conflict in Ukraine serves as a reminder of the difficulties associated with resolving ethnic and territorial disputes in the post-Soviet world.

In addition, it emphasizes the significance of continuing international dialogue and cooperation toward a peaceful conflict resolution.

Chapter 4

The KGB's role in the conflict.

This chapter will look at the KGB's role in the conflict in Eastern Ukraine and the annexation of Crimea. The KGB, or Komitet Gosudarstvennoy Bezopasnosti, was the main intelligence agency of the Soviet Union. It played a significant role in the annexation of Crimea and the ongoing conflict in Eastern Ukraine. We will investigate how KGB tactics, such as disinformation and covert operations, have been used to sow division and advance Russia's objectives.

It is believed that the KGB carried out a variety of covert operations before the annexation of Crimea to destabilize the Ukrainian government and set the stage for Russia to intervene. The financing of pro-Russian groups in Ukraine, the dissemination of false information and propaganda, and the infiltration of Ukrainian security forces were all components of these operations.

Once Russia had annexed Crimea, the KGB's role shifted to supporting pro-Russian separatist forces in Eastern Ukraine. It is believed that the agency engaged in cyber-attacks and disinformation campaigns to further destabilize the region, in addition to providing these groups with military and logistical support.

One key strategy used by the KGB in this conflict has been the dissemination of false information and propaganda. The organization has utilized social media platforms and different channels to spread fake news and misinformation about the conflict, to discredit the Ukrainian government, and justify Russia's actions.

The KGB has also used covert operations, such as sending Special Forces and intelligence agents to support pro-Russian forces on the ground, as another strategy. In addition to carrying out espionage and sabotage operations, these agents have been crucial in assisting and coordinating separatist forces.

The KGB's involvement in the annexation of Crimea and the conflict in Eastern Ukraine shows how Russian intelligence agencies continue to use covert tactics and disinformation to achieve their geopolitical objectives. Even though the agency has been officially taken over by the Federal Security Service (FSB) since the fall of the Soviet Union, its legacy still has an impact on how Russian intelligence is carried out today.

Before Russian troops entered the peninsula in February 2014, the KGB was involved in the annexation of Crimea. The KGB and other Russian intelligence agencies had been working for years to destabilize the Ukrainian government and set the stage for Russia to intervene. This included funding pro-Russian groups in Ukraine, gaining access to Ukrainian security forces, and spreading false information and propaganda.

For instance, disinformation campaigns were used by Russian intelligence agencies to misrepresent the Ukrainian government as a fascist regime that was executing ethnic Russians in Ukraine. The narrative that Russia supported pro-Russian separatist forces in Eastern Ukraine and annexed Crimea was bolstered by this propaganda.

For instance, Russian intelligence operatives have been spotted on the ground in Eastern Ukraine, providing military support and coordinating with pro-Russian separatist forces. These individuals have also been involved in espionage and sabotage, such as the downing of Malaysia Airlines Flight MH17 in July 2014, which was probably carried out by a Russian missile system manned by personnel trained by the KGB.

The KGB's role in the annexation of Crimea and the conflict in Eastern Ukraine highlights the ongoing use of covert tactics and disinformation by Russian intelligence agencies to achieve their geopolitical goals. Even though the agency has been officially taken over by the Federal Security Service (FSB) since the fall of the Soviet Union, its legacy still has an impact on how Russian intelligence is carried out today. In response to advancements in technology, the KGB's strategies, which include covert operations and disinformation, have been improved and modernized, but their fundamental principles have not changed.

Chapter 5

International Response to Putin's War on Ukraine

We'll look at how the world responded to the events in Ukraine. The events in Ukraine, including the annexation of Crimea and the ongoing conflict in Eastern Ukraine, have prompted a variety of international responses from Western nations, the United Nations, and neighboring countries. We will investigate the sanctions imposed by Western nations, the role of the United Nations, and the response of neighboring countries.

In response to Russia's actions in Ukraine, Western nations, such as the United States, the European Union, and Canada, have imposed a variety of economic sanctions on the country. These approvals have targeted key sectors of the Russian economy, including finance, energy, and defense, and have had a significant impact on the Russian economy. Notwithstanding monetary approvals, Western nations have likewise imposed travel bans and asset freezes on Russian officials and individuals believed to be involved in the annexation of Crimea and the conflict in Eastern Ukraine.

The response to the events in Ukraine has also involved the United Nations. A resolution condemning Russia's actions in Crimea and affirming Ukraine's territorial integrity was approved by the UN General Assembly in March 2014. The UN has also deployed a monitoring mission to Ukraine to observe and report on the human rights situation in the country.

The events in Ukraine have been closely monitored by neighboring countries, particularly those with significant Russian-ethnic populations, and different responses have been provided. Belarus, which has generally been a partner of Russia, has to a great extent upheld Russia's activities in Ukraine. Kazakhstan, which has a large Russian-ethnic population, has responded with greater caution, stressing the importance of a diplomatic solution to the conflict. The Baltic states, which have a significant Russian ethnic population and historical ties to Ukraine, have been among the most vocal supporters of Western sanctions and have strongly condemned Russia's actions.

The global response to the events in Ukraine has been mixed. While Western countries have imposed significant economic sanctions on Russia and taken steps to support Ukraine, the conflict in Eastern Ukraine continues to simmer, and there is little consensus on how to resolve the situation. Russia's relations with its neighbors have been strained as a result of the ongoing conflict, which has also contributed to a broader sense of instability and uncertainty in the region.

Some countries have offered Ukraine military support in addition to diplomatic and economic sanctions efforts against Russia. The US, for instance, has given Ukraine a military guide including weapons, ammo, and training for its military forces. In addition, Canada has provided non-lethal military support in the form of communications and body armor.

In response to these international actions, Russia has imposed countersanctions on Western nations and denied any involvement in the conflict in Eastern Ukraine. As a means of countering Western pressure, Russia has also sought to strengthen its alliances with other nations, particularly China.

Regardless of these endeavors, the conflict in Eastern Ukraine keeps on stewing, with periodic outbreaks of violence and no clear path to resolution. The situation has also created a humanitarian crisis, with thousands of people displaced from their homes and in need of aid.

The international response to the events in Ukraine has highlighted the challenges of dealing with a major geopolitical crisis in a highly interconnected world. Economic sanctions and diplomatic efforts can be effective, but they rarely suffice to end complex and prolonged conflicts. The current situation in Ukraine serves as a powerful reminder of the ongoing conflict between competing geopolitical interests and the intricate web of relationships that support international relations.

The fact that the conflict has increased cooperation between Ukraine and other countries in the region, such as Poland and the Baltic states, is one potential positive outcome. These nations have worked to strengthen their defenses against a possible attack by Russia while also providing Ukraine with more support.

Another potential result is that the contention could prompt a reassessment of the job of NATO and the importance of collective security in Europe. NATO's increased presence in the region has contributed to deterring further Russian aggression, and the conflict has highlighted the significance of maintaining a united front against Russian aggression.

However, there is also the possibility that the conflict will result in a more fractured and divisive Europe, with nations pursuing their interests rather than cooperating for the common good. This could make it harder for the region to deal with challenges in the future, like a possible Russian attack or other security threats.

The conflict in Ukraine has, as a whole, had significant and far-reaching effects on Russia, Ukraine, and the world at large. It has brought to light the importance of collective security, the requirement for increased support and cooperation for Ukraine, and the risks posed by aggressive and destabilizing policies pursued by individual nations. As we look to the future, it will be crucial to work toward promoting peace, stability, and cooperation in the region and to learn from the lessons of the conflict.

Chapter six

Conclusion

In conclusion, this book has shed light on the complex and multifaceted nature of the conflict in Ukraine and its implications for the wider world. We have seen how Putin's past as a KGB agent has shaped his leadership style and policies, and how KGB tactics have been used to further Russia's goals.

The annexation of Crimea and Russia's support for separatist rebels in eastern Ukraine have led to increased tensions between Russia and the West, with far-reaching consequences for global security and stability. The ongoing humanitarian crisis in Ukraine has also highlighted the devastating impact of conflict and the urgent need for international cooperation and support.

As we look to the future, it is clear that the conflict in Ukraine will continue to have significant implications for Russia, Ukraine, and the international community. We must continue to learn from the lessons of this conflict and work towards promoting peace, stability, and cooperation in the region.

Ultimately, the events in Ukraine serve as a stark reminder of the dangers of aggressive and destabilizing policies pursued by individual countries and the importance of maintaining a strong and united front against such actions. We hope that this book has provided valuable insights into this important topic and contributed to a deeper understanding of the complexities of the conflict in Ukraine.